The Boston Massacre
Five Colonists Killed By British Soldiers

Allison Stark Draper

The Rosen Publishing Group's
PowerKids Press™
New York

For my father

Published in 2001 by The Rosen Publishing Group, Inc.
29 East 21st Street, New York, NY 10010

Copyright © 2001 by The Rosen Publishing Group, Inc.

First Edition

Book Design: Michael de Guzman

The picture on the cover shows an engraving of the Boston Massacre by Paul Revere.

Photo Credits: p. 5 © National Portrait Gallery, London/SuperStock; p. 6 © North Wind Pictures; pp. 9, 13 by Tim Hall; pp. 10,17, 21 by MaryJane Wojciechowski; p. 14 © CORBIS/Bettmann; p. 18 © SuperStock.

Draper, Allison Stark.
    The Boston Massacre : five colonists killed by British soldiers / by Allison Stark Draper.
      p. cm.— (Headlines from history)
    Includes index.
    Summary: Describes the incidents leading up to the Boston Massacre, the event itself, the trial following it, and its importance in American history.
    ISBN 0-8239-5670-9 (lib.)
    1. Boston Massacre, 1770—Juvenile literature. [1. Boston Massacre, 1770] I. Title. II . Series.
E215 .4 .D7 2000
973.2'7—dc21   99-55230

Manufactured in the United States of America

CONTENTS

American Colonists
Struggle Under British Rule

In the early 1600s, British **settlers** sailed from England to America. Some of these settlers landed in Massachusetts. They founded a town called Boston.

In the 1700s, the settlers were ruled by King George III of England. They paid British taxes and obeyed British laws. As time passed, the British settlers stopped thinking of themselves as British **citizens**. They started to think of themselves as American **colonists**. By the late 1700s, many Americans were angry that they were still ruled by the British.

On March 5, 1770, a fight broke out at the Custom House in Boston. Five American colonists were shot and killed by British soldiers. The Americans named this event the Boston **Massacre**.

King George III of England did not want the American colonists to rule themselves.

American Boy Shot
in Anti-British Demonstration

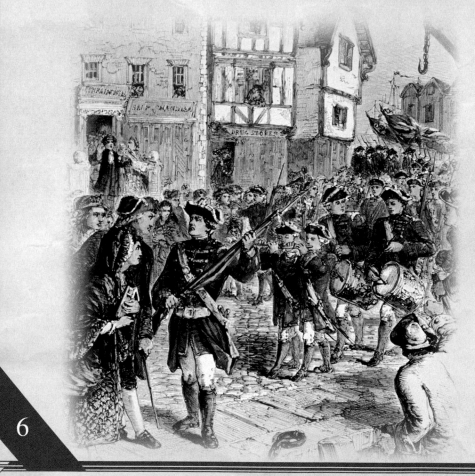

The British knew that most Americans did not want to follow British laws. They sent soldiers to Boston to scare the Americans.

 British soldiers tried to keep the American colonists under control.

6

British soldiers armed with guns stood guard all over Boston. This made the American colonists even angrier. They did not like being treated as enemies.

One morning in February 1770, a crowd of angry Americans surrounded the house of a man named Ebenezer Richardson who sided with the British. They threw rocks at his windows. A rock shattered the glass and hit his wife.

Mr. Richardson fired his **musket** into the crowd. He killed an 11-year-old boy named Christopher Snider. Hundreds of Americans attended the boy's funeral. Many blamed the British for his death.

7

British Soldier Fights
With American Rope Maker

On March 2, 1770, a British soldier went to a rope yard to ask for work. William Green, one of the rope makers, said the soldier could clean his outdoor bathroom.

The British soldier was insulted. The two men fought and the soldier lost. He left, but returned with several soldiers and started the fight again. William Green and the other rope makers won. The British soldiers left, then returned with even more men. The owner of the rope yard came out and stopped the fight. He told the British soldiers to go home.

The soldiers were still angry. Later on, an American overheard a British soldier's wife say that soon the soldiers would "wet their **bayonets** in New England people's blood."

After an American rope maker insulted a British soldier, a fight broke out between the two men.

9

American Colonists Attack British Guard

On March 5, 1770, a British soldier named Hugh White stood guard on King Street. Hugh White was a **private** in

10

the British army. He was guarding the street alone. Several American boys gathered to make fun of him.

More American colonists arrived. Soon, a crowd of 50 people were yelling at Private White. Private White did not want any trouble. He tried to stand still and ignore them. Then a teenaged boy named Edward Garrick touched Private White's uniform. Private White lifted his musket and hit the boy in the face.

The crowd of Americans screamed. They threw rocks and ice at Private White. They told him they would kill him. Someone rang a fire alarm bell and more Americans came. Private White yelled for help.

Private White tried to ignore the American boys who were teasing him.

11

American Mob Faces
Captain Preston and Soldiers

Two British soldiers heard Private White yell for help. The soldiers ran to the British guard station at the end of the street. The officer in charge was Captain Thomas Preston. Captain Preston and eight soldiers marched out to help Private White.

Captain Preston ordered his soldiers to carry their muskets but not to fire them. The soldiers stayed close together. They used their sharp bayonets to push through the crowd. The Americans threw snowballs at Preston and his men.

The soldiers were surrounded. The crowd grew larger. The Americans yelled insults at the soldiers. They called them lobsters because of their red coats.

12   *The British soldiers pushed their way through the crowd of angry Americans.* 👈

13

British-American Shoot-Out at Custom House

14

Captain Preston stood in front of his men to keep them from firing. He told the Americans to go home. One of the Americans threw a huge stick at the soldiers. It hit a British soldier in the face and knocked him down.

The British soldier got to his feet. He lifted his musket and fired into the crowd. Everyone froze. Then, the Americans rushed forward to attack the British soldiers.

Three or four British soldiers fired their guns. The Americans fought back with sticks and rocks. The British soldiers kept firing. They shot a total of 11 men. One of the men the soldiers shot was an American merchant named Edward Payne. Another was an American sailor named Crispus Attucks.

After an American threw a stick at a British soldier, the soldier fired into the crowd.

15

Eleven Americans Shot
by British Soldiers

On the night of March 5, 1770, Captain Preston's British soldiers fired 10 or 12 shots at the mob of American colonists. They killed three Americans on the spot. Two Americans were **fatally** injured and died shortly afterward. Six Americans were wounded.

After the shooting, the Americans gathered up the dead and wounded men and carried them back to their families. They sent for doctors and spread the news of the massacre.

Captain Preston marched his soldiers home to their **barracks**. At 2:00 A.M. on March 6, the town sheriff arrested Captain

16

If they were found guilty of murder, Captain Preston and his men would be put to death.

Preston. He charged Preston and eight of his men with murder. If they were found guilty, they would be put to death.

17

American Lawyer John Adams Defends British Soldiers

The Boston Massacre was a confusing event. Some Americans believed that the British soldiers were murderers.

In 1797, John Adams would become the second president of the United States.

18

Others, like future president John Adams, were worried the massacre would lead to more violence.

John Adams was a lawyer and an American **patriot** before he was elected president. He believed in justice for all people. In the case of the Boston Massacre, he believed that the British soldiers had fired in **self-defense**. He thought that the soldiers had the right to protect themselves from an angry mob, even if that mob had a right to be angry at the British. John Adams decided to **defend** Captain Preston and his soldiers at their trial.

19

British Soldiers Found Not Guilty of Boston Massacre

The trial of the British soldiers started on October 24, 1770. Many people **testified**. Everyone remembered the night differently. One American said there were only 70 Americans in the street. He said they were angry but not dangerous. He said Preston's soldiers attacked them with bayonets.

Captain Preston said that there were 400 Americans on King Street that night. He said that they threatened to murder the British soldier on guard.

John Adams proved that the soldiers fired to save their own lives. On October 31, 1770, Captain Preston was found not

John Adams proved that the British soldiers had fired their guns in self-defense.

guilty and released from jail. All of the British soldiers were found not guilty of murder. Two were found guilty of **manslaughter**.

Colonists Make First Move Toward Independence

The Boston Massacre was an important step toward the American Revolution and the creation of the United States of America. It convinced many Americans that they should not be ruled by the British.

An American patriot named Paul Revere made an engraving of the Boston Massacre. The **engraving** shows a row of British soldiers firing on unarmed Americans. People who had not been at the massacre were horrified by the picture. It made them think differently about the British. Some became determined to drive the British out of America forever.

22

GLOSSARY

barracks (BAYR-iks) The buildings where soldiers live.

bayonets (BAY-oh-nets) Long sharp swords attached to the barrels of guns.

citizens (SIH-tih-zens) People who are born in or have the legal right to live in a certain country.

colonists (KAH-luh-nists) People who live in a colony.

defend (dih-FEND) To take someone's side in an argument.

engraving (en-GRAY-ving) A designer picture that is cut into wood, stone, metal, or glass plates for printing.

fatally (FAY-tul-lee) Ending in death.

manslaughter (MAN-slaw-ter) To kill a person in self-defense or by accident.

massacre (MAS-uh-ker) A fight in which many people on one side are killed.

musket (MUS-kit) A gun with a long barrel used in battle and hunting.

patriot (PAY-tree-ot) A person who loves and defends his or her country.

private (PRY-vit) A type of soldier in the army.

self-defense (SELF-dih-FENS) To protect yourself against an attack.

settlers (SEH-tuh-lerz) People who move to a new land to live.

testified (TES-tih-fyed) To have spoken in court about the facts of a trial.

INDEX

WEB SITES

To learn more about the Boston Massacre, check out these Web sites:

24

http://www.beavton.k12.or.us/Barnes/revwarreport/bostonmassacre.html#report
http://www.shawneenet.com/political_science/v3boston.htm